IN THE MUSEUM OF
MISREMEMBERED THINGS

Linda McKenna

Doire Press

First published in 2020

Doire Press
Aille, Inverin
Co. Galway
www.doirepress.com

Layout: Lisa Frank
Cover design: Tríona Walsh
Cover art: Artur Balytskyi / shutterstock.com
Odua Images / shutterstock.com
Author photo: Peadar Curran

Printed by Clódóirí CL
Casla, Co. na Gaillimhe

ISBN 978-1-907682-76-6

We gratefully acknowledge the assistance of The Arts Council of Northern Ireland.

LOTTERY FUNDED

CONTENTS

For Christopher

In the Museum of Misremembered Things

the keeper writes a slanted hand;
fine nibbed copperplate tracking

imagined lines of pink and blue.
In lemon juice; this archive

of unprovenanced vows, misheard
names, missed cues. Some day

she may rip out the pages, lay
them flat, heat up the iron. For now,

invisible; the lover picking out
her name on snow so white,

it looked like truth; unbending
wedding lilies, pearls for sorrow,

tangled lace. She leaves space
for days and dates; mislaid,

or folded small, in drawers
of long sold, white-lined boxes.

Unsettled

The builders swear the cracks
are settlement; will settle. May
even in time close. They don't.
Widening, they let in wraiths
of Grand Duchesses, demanding
to be fed on eggs and cream,
fattened back to dimples.

Their gloves never white enough,
they throw off the crazy pieced
patchwork, bruise themselves
on makeshift fences, scratch
themselves on young hedges;
having never known unwrapped
corners, thorns, hidden tree stumps.

In the Dalldorf Asylum Clara Peuthert
is reading a map of silver scars.
Elsewhere, a boy cuts himself
to prove he cannot stop bleeding.
Every day plaster crumbles under
nervous fingers, every day more
visible, the rag stuffed wattle daub.

Overpainted

After The Massacre of the Innocents *by Pieter Bruegel the Elder*

Some journeyman. Out of his apprenticeship.
Skilful enough to make the brush as sharp

as a nib drawing the tricky edges of feathers,
detail of claws. Softening it for curves and cloth.

Good with colour; knowing a splash of red holds
the eye, hides what shouldn't be seen. Under no

illusion he can match the master's incomparable
northern skies, in places thin to transparency;

in others the thickly layered threat of more snow.
The peculiar fluorescence in spreading grey slush;

the precise folds of shawl, careless lacing of shirts.
Neither did he touch the roofs, tucked in white

blankets tasselled with icicles. A child becomes
a pitcher; richly glazed, about to be broken.

A bundle unravelling from its bands of string;
a calf, big-eyed and trusting; a boar, squealing,

scrabbling but in the end, easily caught. In piles,
they are magicked into turkeys, still incongruous

and exotic; prosaic, local geese. Except in a
dark doorway where he leaves two; one dangling

from a soldier's hand. And the girl, offered now
in place of a swan.

Witness Statements

They rise up in copperplate the long dead,
with an elegance and sinuous grace they
lacked in life. Ragged lines straightened,
crooked columns shuffled together;
lower case shoulders, upper case pikes.

They emerge as if from the same hand,
identically stately, invisible margins exactly
the same width, as if some ancient, holy scribe,
his writing box and quill under his arm,
had cast some magical spell over the land.

But of course it is the hand that is inherited.
Passed down from darned and patched tutors,
clergymen with no livings, to these junior officers,
shaking out their cramping fingers, careful
not to blot the pages of life and death.

The witnesses process neatly across the page,
released from byre and shed; brushed and
combed for the day. Their carefully laid out,
careless actions; lounging against a neighbour's
wall at midnight, travelling miles to borrow a rake,

and squeezed small between the marching
lines of traitors and curves of smoke, some
women, who are reminded what an oath
means, and told to speak loud and be sure
to repeat exactly what they heard the men saying.

One Year On

The trees hug their wounds
tight, shed skin with leaves;

give out flowers of flame.
But the hills, being old, stretch;

pull the sun lower in the sky;
so the town, gap-toothed,

rawly pink, squints out of
puffed-up eyes; thinks it sees

ghosts moving in the sodden
fields, scrabbling up bones.

No doubt what's left of strayed
sheep, or the remains of giants

who fed on thorns and nettles;
followed false gods, hauled huge

rocks into the shape of altars,
had odd ways of burying their dead.

A Code for After

By ballot this battle scene.
The hills are considered very
like. You are invited to find
yourself, the key being lost.

I was about my business.
The latching of the barn door,
the milking of the cow,
the shoeing of the horse.

By ballot my name came out,
I took bread and buttermilk.
My wife gave me a pocket-book,
with a needle and thread.

The colours of rebellion
are green-yellow grass turning
brown with, here and there,
a fraying ribbon of rose.

I think about my quilt.
How the back will be
the faded striped ticken
that is still sturdy and strong.

The pieces will be slanted
rectangles of blue, yellow,
red; anchored by a double
border of feather stitches.

After, I sewed up my pockets,
of copper pennies, scraps
of ribbons, petals of dog roses;
went back to my farm,

the milking of the cow,
the shoeing of the horse.
On the way, a bright guinea
fell from a magpie's nest.

(Thomas Romney Robinson's painting of the battle of Ballynahinch was sold by ballot. There was a key to the people shown which got lost. Militia companies were raised by ballot. In the eighteenth and nineteenth centuries some soldiers made quilts to pass the time between engagements.)

Ceremonial

We are over a line none of us can see,
but the chart and compass say *now*. So

we sprinkle fresh water on the sea, blessing
our arrival in the other half of the world.

Neptune wears a battered crown, carries
a blunt fork for a trident. The mermaid,

legs bound together, is the ship's carpenter;
stuffed into the stinking skin of a porpoise,

cheeks reddened, careful with his ringlets
of wood shavings. At a distance, porpoises

look smooth and sleek. Close to, they are
pitted and scarred. You think they will swim

underneath the ship, topple us out, either side
of the line. I have seen other things; the fleet

of gulls that followed for days until we were
too far from where they scavenge; a body

sewn neatly into canvas, sliding into the sea;
a woman gathering up the skeins of her hair,

plaiting them, sewing the plaits into her cap.
Another wearing the wooden jacket, stumbling

against the swell of the waves, feet scrabbling
for balance, which amused us for a while.

(Sailors performed a ceremony acknowledging 'King Neptune' as their ships crossed the Equator.)

Christmas Day on the 'Lord Sidmouth', 1823

Somewhere along the old slave coast, Martha Edwards,
swaddled in a blanket, laid in a canvas bag, slid into
the sea. One of twins, the other dead two weeks;
victims of bad nursing and bad living. Further south
Robert Borsch fell overboard. No pause to search
for a boy well-grown and boisterous, bound to be
a burden on the fragile colony, its delicately balanced
economy. Instead the ship ploughed on to where
the stars are upside down, frost the wrong way round.
Mustered on the boiling deck, the female cargo mumbled
along to a dimly familiar story: ox, ass, something
about a journey, something about salvation. Then lined
up for the indulgent half-pint of wine served to every
woman, bond or free, this being Christmas Day.

*(The 'Lord Sidmouth' was a convict ship. The National Archives, UK, hold the medical
journals kept by the ships' Surgeon Superintendents.)*

That Last Thing

They belong to the air. Know
the time by dandelion clocks;
the feather thieves. Light-fingered,
bird-boned. Slashing at pillows,
swooping on warehouses;
hawking *strippings* and *drivings*,
the very refuse of feathers.

At the Cape of Good Hope,
the ships pause, take on fresh
fruit, pass it among the cargo;
robbers of gates and grates,
fire irons and plated candlesticks.
The feather thieves peck
at oranges, feel the air thickening,

watch the skies shifting; untangle
their hair, face south. In Newgate,
Elizabeth Flinn, *ten pounds worth
of ostrich plumes, sentence death*,
blows a stray feather; marvels
at its faint flutter, its hopeful,
irresistible mimicry of flight.

Resting Place

'May your Excellency... mitigate this Sentence so that their Bones may be laid
in a homely grave ...'

—*The Convict Petition of Mary and Ann Atcheson, 1827*

This thin soil hoards its goodness
a pinch here and there, enough
for foraging sheep, enough to nudge
the whins to dance yellow, enough
to warm the half-asleep hills.

This narrow water lies silver and cold,
the mist rising and staying all day
in your hair, on your clothes; wool
never drying, feet always gripping
over seaweed strewn rocks.

This land grudges its harvests, hides
away riches, rewards patient hands;
the skin opening and bleeding,
cutting and cleaving the closed tight
shells. Inside, life plumping and pulsing.

(Convict petition, PPC 3259, National Archives of Ireland.)

Mission

I am becoming very absent, much
unfitted for the affairs of this life,
reclaimed from the bog, twenty-six
more acres to be tilled. In my dreams,
the clack of the loom, stamp of the press,

God the Weaver, God the Printer
busying Himself with lengths of sturdy
homespun; turning the wrong way
round letters right on the page so
we all can sing, anam, slánú, súil, solas.

Patient with my vanity, mórchúis;
choosing the best frocks which in any
case will rot, and cannot compare
with the white gowns of salvation
He has laid out for my babes.

I pick the one ruffled at the neck,
the one embroidered with daisies,
the one with lace from my wedding dress.
Edward has been much spared in this,
owing to his absence from home.

(The quotations in italics at the beginning and end are from a letter written in 1837,
by Eliza Nangle, wife of Rev. Edward Nangle, who founded 'the Mission' at Dugourt,
Achill. The Mission published its own hymn book and prayer book in Irish, established
schools and built houses. Three of Eliza's children died as babies during the time of the
Mission.)

Reclaimed

'The Dead were Anna, Helena, Hugh, Jane and Archibald, being all God's
Lovely Loans.'
   —Walter Harris, *The Antient and Present State of the County of Down*, 1744

Feather-light, or standing surprised
on their own two feet, the lovely
loans are reclaimed back to sleep,
stowed for eternity in God's pocket,

and we pray hard to believe that
now they are sparrows and lilies;
swaddled in shawls of silver,
outshining even Solomon,

that all those others, stitched
into cheap linen, wrapped in plastic,
interred in the bodies of dead
mothers, will share in the fading

carved gifts of Anna's eyes,
Helena's strong grip, Hugh's smile,
Jane, the wriggler, always on the move,
Archibald laughing at his own hiccup.

Heart Sore

'Schroder affirms that some Persons hang the Heart of this Bird about the Neck of Children to cure the Falling sickness.'
—Walter Harris, *The Antient and Present State of the County of Down*, 1744

How long to follow this *shy*
and *most solitary* of birds.
How solitary you must
become yourself; far beyond
the reach of friend and home.

Then, the wait for the prize
of the heart; the glass going
backwards and forwards,
examining every inch of this
most perfect structure.

The endless scratch of the pen
searching for the precise
word to conjure the colour
of the wings; *shining vivid
green, azure spots.*

The days of measuring
and drawing, erasing, measuring
again; then the paint to be
mixed just so, thinly applied.
Only then the cut.

In such despair I would prefer
the stomach, lined with tiny
bones and scales. The bones
would strengthen, the scales
cover and warm;

my silvered child would
be both bird and fish; never
fall without flying, never
drown; make his way surely
over any sharp rock.

Play in the foam of the sea,
that some say the Kingfisher
spins into her nest, where
her young, waiting for her return,
open their yellow mouths.

Antient and Present

'She was alive the year King Charles was beheaded and says she is 95 or 96 years old. She keeps a school for Children.'
—Walter Harris, *The Antient and Present State of the County of Down*, 1744

The women scour the trees of blood,
rinse the rivers clean, rake the bones
into dark corners; set to the men's
work of sowing, weeding, reaping.
Binding sheaves with plaits of straw
and hair plucked from rotting corpses.

In spring the world marches green
and yellow; the men emerge, tender
with their wounds, cradling babies
and kindling. Clucking over crooked
drills and unmarked boundaries, they
find the whet stones, sharpen blades.

The women turn to their prayer books,
and Bibles, rip out the blank pages,
trim goose feathers into quills;
open penny-schools to teach, *a stitch
in time saves nine, no rose without
a thorn, pride goeth before a fall.*

Salt

'Great dearth of salt this year…so much so that the jesting folk were composing its elegy.'

— The Annals of Ulster

The acrobats are balancing on the barrels
where we used to store winter, brimming
with salty treasure: pork, beef, venison, cod.
Even the children don't clamour to stop,
dragging on their mothers' hands, perching
on the ground to stare. We are busy being
crammed with the spoils of the hunt, the cuts
of the animals too tired to stay alive. As fat
bellied as ships sent to relieve a siege, our flesh
so rich, so dense, famine's teeth will break
before they reach our bones. The dishes scowl
unscoured on careless tables where strangers'
elbows jostle and poke. The whipped boys
are wearing ribbons of rotting flesh.

Naoise at the Chip Shop

The lough is always a silver ribbon,
the road always a grey. The boy

is ribboned in blood, red and pink,
the edges fraying like the chewed

ends of our schooldays. Bare white
chest, closed tight sky, red against

white against grey. He halts us
in our gasping circuit; holy well,

stone church, workhouse, carpet
warehouse. We stop for the story;

glass at his feet, the policewoman
folding him into her arms. Crows

swoop on chips swelling in oily
puddles, peck in small-eyed judgement,

move on. We move on, we know
the story, how it unwinds; treachery

and tears, a long, forced journey.
Some girl waiting, tent pitched

on a hillside, a shouldering of small
bundles. At the end, his mother,

whose name no-one remembers,
whose sorrows no-one retells.

Glass Dress

The glass dress hangs in the wooden
barn. Warms itself by what daylight

and moonlight leeches through gaps
in the walls. Sometimes the glass dress

is a mirror. But it never gives back
what we want to see: sheet music,

box irons, silver sixpences. Instead,
by moonlight, it shows us our hands,

always washing themselves of blame
from a variety of basins; gold, pewter,

stainless steel, dried fingers thimbled
against the prick of conscience.

By daylight, those same hands sign
away our ancestors, loop rope over

trees. The glass dress will not show us
before and after, only here and here.

So it becomes deserted, swallowed
by couch grass and nettles. The barn

splinters around the glass dress.
It could be used to house cattle, store

ploughs, but it goes on in its thankless
task of shelter, profiting no one.

Baking Day

Today is the day I make bread,
my hands mimicking her grace
and speed, knead, stretch, pat
knead, pinch and shape, the same
loaves she loved us with.

Today is the day God and I call
a truce. He nods across the chasm
between us, I dust the bread with
her prayers, trusting he will see
the dough rise, golden and fragrant.

We eat it with Aunt Sofie's plum jam
her envy-of-the-street, see-if-you
can-beg-the recipe-off-her jam, the
spicy-sweet spoonfuls of autumn
my sisters and I stole.

God and I having resumed our
normal hostilities, my grace
is one of my brother's trip-me-up
riddles, 'what weighs more, a tonne
of iron or a tonne of feathers?'

The Colouring of Eggs

The little broken houses. Bluer
than the sky, the virgin's cloak,
newborn nurseries. So blue
they make a new name,
are carried away.
To confuse predators,
stop the tiny, ugly babies
from injuring themselves,
keep the place clean.
Or the mother bird eats them
to replenish calcium.
The blue was made last
in the long day it took
to build the egg and
comes from biliverdin,
which also makes bile;
the stuff of vomit and anger.

Take in the bitter with
the calcium, you will need it.
So many of these babies
will never make it;
will never put on weight
or feathers, will fall
into cats' mouths, will freeze.
Maybe better your plundered
ancestors lying in careful
nested drawers in guilty
unvisited corners.
I count 212 in the varnished
cabinets; keyless music boxes
whose song I can't shake off.

Delivery Day

We saw death being delivered today.
Polished and gleaming like any piece
of new furniture, but like unhoused
furniture faintly indecent. And startlingly
unprotected. No layers of foam, corners
of cardboard that we use to stop sofas
and bookcases from bruising each other.

Death was surprisingly narrow and
insubstantial looking; casually unloaded
from a shabby blue van, by men in jeans
and sweatshirts, who blocked the pavement
where we stopped; surprised out of our
spiteful office gossip, unsure whether
to laugh or bless ourselves.

Charlatans

We knew the trick; learned the trick
in rigged-up darkrooms, giggling girls

in sheets. Then death tricked us, rigged
us out in jet and weeds; edged all our days

with black. We called on angels, wings
strapped down, to summon back the dear

departed; from behind the ticking clocks;
abide with me, the lost ring has slipped

between two loose floor boards in the back
bedroom. We knew the trick, but tricked

ourselves with proof; the ring emerged
filmed in grease and dust. Now the ghosts

are loose, in the back bedroom, telling
human stories, playing cards for matchsticks.

They won't go back, the tricky ghosts;
breaking antique brooches, tapping messages

we can't make out, looking every day more
and more like they might vanish us.

A Girl Goes Out

Ismene: 'The toil and trouble, father, that I bore…I spare thee.'
— *Oedipus at Colonus*, Sophocles

You have the best props,
a sleek colt, a low brimmed
sun bonnet, but in this unmothered
world, the worst words,
a mother's words: *wait,*
wait and see, wait it out.

A girl stays, a girl goes out.
Into a world that is a river;
stubborn, determined to empty
itself into the sea; where
there is a dam, it stops,
waits, seeps its way through.

There is no chorus to chant
the way. The skies are
unreadable, the stars fickle.
Birdsong means nothing,
only, here is morning,
keep away from my nest.

The world picks flesh
from bony fish, salts
its thin porridge, chews
herbs to stave off hunger;
while it carts pomegranates
and figs to the greedy city.

The world prizes horseflesh
over womanflesh. A horse
can be trained to a plough,
raced for silver. How many times
do you lie down on oily wool
to keep its hands from the colt?

The world is not the city but
the town. Shrieking its wares,
burning out its neighbours,
insisting that none of its ancestral
laws be written; so a stranger
never knows why he is to hang.

At the frantic end of summer,
the fairground plays the smallest
town. Fortunes are dearer but
meaner; the tall stranger not
so handsome, the cat by the fire,
flea-ridden; some children will die.

And as the cart drivers might
have told you, the best thing
to do is to *wait, wait and see
wait it out*, not flee until your house
is burned to the ground, know
the gods will not rebuild it.

But you go back, hands cupped
around a fools' tale, careful
not to spill a drop. On the way
you stop, pull down your sun
bonnet, brush the colt's coat,
lead him over the narrowing way.

Ismene (Aside)

The city is swayed by words, cries
over the barefoot, sunburnt girl,

takes up its quill; changes the chorus.
And this is where I will be buried;

a footnote, small printed quibble,
briefly dragging the eye to the bottom

of the page, intruding on the principal
action. A what-if, on the other hand,

or lesser view hanging dismissable,
over the page where you, my always

spotlit sister are centred, weaving golden
circles of verse with the skill other girls

loop ribbons, twist wool. The lines
flowing on from each other, a pattern

we have to follow to the end, then
go back and read again, then say out loud.

The words individual pieces of bright
glass dropping onto the stage, glowing

where they fall, singing in our heads,
on the street, so we repeat them as vows,

as ritual. Behind the curtain I sweep up
the dust, wonder, how will we live now?

Ismene Heads North

where girls, sewn into wolfskin,
paint red through the forest.

In the long night time she pays
the gods their due; swallows

black bread and herring, prays
a litany of save us. The summer

days she keeps for herself, eats
sun-warmed raspberries; watches

the dust motes swirl heedlessly
to the ground; dreams of witches

and woodcutters whose axes
slice through stone and bone,

entrails and ice; dragging bloody
mouthed princesses reluctantly to life.

The Better Part

(i) Ruth/Orpah

Unlike me, you kept your dowry
untarnished; ironed your veils
crisp, polished pots and plates,
shielded carpets from the sun.
So now you put off widowhood,
with a tinkling of bright bells
on the waxed, supple leather
of your horse's reins and bridle.

I laid mine out for pleasure;
stained pewter with orange
and yellow spices, smashed
clay flasks to get at the sweetness
within. Wore my best on workdays,
slept naked and perfumed on
expensive linen meant for
shrouds and childbed.

What's left is my new mother,
all fragile bones, barely enough
of her to fill a cradle, but like
any hungry baby her grip is fierce,
her cries loud. To soothe her
I take out my broken wedding
words. Yes stay, yes cleave,
yes, one God, one land, one grave.

(ii)   Martha/Mary

Our mother would have said indecorous,
indecent; the careless loosening of the
thick braid of hair, as if it were not her
crowning glory but a servant's broom.
And lazy; she would yawn her way to bed,
leaving the sticky mass unwashed, the
expensive ointment making yellow stains
on her nightgown, pillowcases and sheets.

But in a day of waste; spilled wine, ovens
left on for too long, the trodden-in bread;
it is the waste of oil for one small lamp
that makes me draw the water first too hot,
then too cold. Makes my fingers thorns, raking
through her hair; my mouth full of nettles
blistering her with scorn, that to my shame
she receives with something like grace.

Joan

We would burn.
The flames would catch us careless,
preening in the glass, cleave
our nylon nightdresses to our flesh.
Their tiny flowers and lace conflagrate;
teach us a lesson.
Our dolls hid their singed hair
under knitted hats; still we couldn't
resist the lure of poker and tongs,
behind adult backs turning
and turning the coal over, exploding
stars into the soot, urging logs to open
their hot red hearts.

She hung beside the mirror.
Eyes closed, shorn boy's head
flung back in ecstasy; a dark
shock against the swirling
grey clouds. Her woollen dress
would have been slower to catch fire.
Did it feel insubstantial on her shoulders
braced for the weight of metal
and leather? Did she smooth
out its creases, shake out the dust,
practise once again walking in it;
shortening her stride, praying
not to stumble?

Elizabeth

Tuck your skirts around your borders
so no skin shows. So no one can see
that you are made of flesh and blood,
and bone, not iron, timber, stone.
Let your body ebb and flow with your rivers,
your streams. Not the dishonest moon
collapsing you in tears, opening you in need.
Be inviolate: beyond the hands and breath
of men, *Insula,* nursed by your cold,
chaste seas. Crave no babe filling your womb,
stirring your milk, for how can you be replicated
except in oil and ink? Keep your self secret
and small, as one of the pins fastening
the cloths that bind your breasts.
Encase yourself in whalebone, sapphire, ivory.
So their eyes squint and fall, their heads lower,
waiting for your glance, your command.
This race you have grown in quarries, pits
and fields. All heart and stomach
and shuttered souls.

Charlotte

It seeps under the door, her narrow
world. Sodden sticks that never light,
tang of manure and straw.
The breaths she takes harsh, rattling.
Like the first shock of rain, so hard
you think it will break glass, splinter
your flesh. Muck smell on the dress
she won't change, the boots dragging
around the table, fists now claws;
those man's fists that punched impartially.

Clay still on the potatoes she guards
but won't eat; small famine eyes
staring. Her eyes narrower, narrower.
But in sunlight the child looks out,
possessive, whining; not fair.
Seeking those other bloody-handed
children, maggoty corpses of birds
and rabbits draped around their necks.
I will make this kitchen clean and cold,
eat only shop-bought bread.

Dispossessed

These are the things I wish
I'd learnt; how to darn a patch
against the wind, braid my new
grown hair into a rope, make a meal
of alms; relish the gristle, ignore
the taint. Bind boughs together
to roof the crazily standing pillars,
one still showing half the face
of a cherub, forgive the day its length,
the night its depth, stop listening
for the rustle that precedes a chant,
harvest tears for salt.

A Weighing

'…with Rooms also for Grand Juries, Petty Juries and Juries of Matrons.'
  —Walter Harris, *The Antient and Present State of the County of Down*, 1744

(i) Intact

As discreet as Justice herself, as blind, using
only the skill of our hands on the secret parts
of the property; we affirm the property
to be intact, can pass to better husbanding.

The land in acres, roods and perches, fields
ploughed and in grass. The livestock:
heifers, calves and cattle in calf. The sheep,
and the hundredweights of wool in bales.

The leases with their bright red clots of sealing
wax; the rental income from houses and shops.
The plantation possessions: male, female, child
and the female with child. What's out at sea,

or if at the bottom, well-insured; and the personal
paraphernalia, held in trust by the property:
necklaces, bracelets, rings. With the exception
of the one, mistakenly called a wedding ring.

(ii) Reprieve

Don't say strawberries, green apples,
cress; say mulberries, cherries, chalk
and coals. Don't say flutter or feather,
for any stomach may flutter with fear,
any heart feather with hope. Say wings.
Not the delicate lace wing of the finch
or the wren, but the ragged, dirt-spattered
wing of gull, pigeon or crow. Say beat;
even drum beat and above all say settle.
The rough, ragged wings have beaten
and clattered their way past your ribs;
now they fold and settle. The quick child
slows, to fatten and float, contemplate
her new soul, the soul pledge of her mother.

Anchor and Anchor

The cloister folds itself in,
a closed accordion of stacked
pleats; sharp pressed edge
to sharp pressed edge.

Tomorrow the day's wings
will gather in battlefield
stumps and mouldy barley,
disobedient daughters, debt.

Now is the time for the soul
facing window, a narrow
point of lamplight where
God swoops and soars.

And behind the door so secret
it can hardly be seen, yawning
narrow-sleeved girls wait,
goffering irons in hand.

Bit Part

Through days of flesh, days of fish,
bitter lettuce, glut of almonds;
Potiphar's wife watches, her grip
eternally loosening on Joseph
fleeing her smooth as silk carnality.

She knows when the scent of lemons
rises, unbearable; at least one novice
will run off for a wife, then abandon
the wife for the market place, for
what is salvation if not prosperity?

O God, see my barns well stocked
for winter, my precise drills, my
neat clipped hedges. Look over
my account books; my additions,
my subtractions. Bless me, bless me.

She knows her beauty is the profit
on peppers and people; that she is
just the aperitif to the meat of the
lean and fat cattle; that what women
think is romance is always a parable.

*(The monks' refectory in the Jeronimos Monastery in Lisbon is decorated with ceramic
tiles depicting the biblical story of Joseph. The monastery's construction and decoration
was funded by a 'pepper tax' on goods coming from Portugal's overseas empire.)*

Not Brothers

Late at night the old West dusts
off its sepia heroes and villains,

and I discover that Billy the Kid
was not the youngest brother

of Frank and Jesse James; did not
die in a gunfight at the OK Corral

as the boys in our school played.
Tarnished guns in homemade

holsters, they opened their veins
with compasses and penknives,

pressed the delicate, pale wrists
together, swore allegiance for ever.

Until the next week, when a new
loyalty unpicked the scabs and

eventually they were all blood
brothers. We envied this game,

already knowing our undying
loves would be undone by differently

shed blood, the drape of veil,
garlands of rose, and milk and milk.

Middle Child

Perfect in the perfect place you always find,
you float effortlessly, as symmetrical as a star,
as skilful as a silver fish that is really a princess.

Suspended in the waves as if caught by the silken
ropes the pantomime fairy flies on, we,
underneath gaping at her skill, her daring.

But yours is no illusion, just another of the easy
accomplishments you offer to us, who bookend
you, begin and end, but never complete you.

We, striking out for the white waves beyond the
warning signs, swimming on until we are rescued,
salty and scarred and sobbing.

Or cowering at the edge, where the sand clings
and clogs like mud, sunburnt flesh stinging,
unblessed by the weightless, healing sea.

Never recognising the middle for what it is;
not too hot or too cold, not too big or too small,
the just right where all fairytale sisters should live.

Annexed

'…we shall annex an Account of Men eminent for their useful Invention, Learning or Promotions.'
　　—Walter Harris, *The Antient and Present State of the County of Down*, 1744

Then dispositions, like diseases, were heritable.
We lived among the notional and flighty, those
who wore their hand-me-down bad luck easily;
and the gifted, tea leaf readers, predictors of rain,

the early riser waking us for the Holyhead boat,
the wheel-of-fortune spinner without whom,
no garden fete could start, the man who docked
the tails of all our pups. In their mouths, a world

of dying words: speckless, tay, conacre. Sometimes
I try them out; nostalgia, faint echo, something false.
Here is a coat with not a brack on it, and that drunk
outside Starbucks, look at the slew of him.

Bringing the News

Gosthering my grandmother called it.
Tights off, skirts rolled up, thighs sprawled

on prim kitchen chairs; the long summer
evening unrolling limply from licked clean

bowls of ripe strawberries mashed with
sugar and the top off the milk. She glared

windows shut in disapproval when the
chief gostherer reported for duty. On parade

from door jamb to door jamb, dripping
the honey of 'you'd never think it' into

sleepy ears, her scraps of Sweet Afton
scented news, whispering under the

battlefield shrieks of scabbed and
ribbonless children, jumping off bales

in the field that anchored our crescent
of houses. She had pulled herself together;

clean smock over elastic waistbanded skirt
unearthed from the wardrobe after weeks

of hopeless finger-crossing, claiming red
cheeks as sunburn, adamant there's always

someone worse off than yourself.

East

I walk two circles here and there. Venn diagram
of my now and then homes, intersections

of church and cricket ground, gatehouses;
useful hedgerows allowed run to seed.

Nettles don't grow here without dock leaves,
thorns are packed with blackberries,

and rose hips. For this is East. Pale and paler
still. Planned, squared off, knowing its place.

Congregating around a ruined abbey, a restored
castle, a sharp diamond. Straightening haphazard

paths and hills, damming water, taming lush
Australian plants with cold and fog. I cherish this.

Not for me the wrecked and wild west, houses
backing into the sea, inviting flood and pirate;

the gaps in talk you fall foolishly into, the tiny
children's walls, fencing off nothing, everything,

especially a grievance. But this securely pinned
and sewn tight Norman world. Its shrewd saints

and maiden ghosts; who rise unsurprised, out
of weathered tombs, only when required.

In the Bones

In the east the first people
dug with bones; scapula of
cow and deer. Leaning in,
shoulder to shoulder,
planting grain, rice,
shallow rooted things.

The bone spades turned
earth from the pit beneath.
Layers where no one yet
rested; bare of shell,
seed, arrowhead.
Nothing but pure clay

and unmarked stone.
The bones being tender
left hardly any trace, nothing
more than a faint childhood
graze, briefly cried over,
soon kissed better.

I dig with my grandfather's
spade; shoulder against
smooth handle, feeling
his wiry strength. This
plants roses, digs in compost,
sometimes lifts coal.

It has outlived his scarred,
consumptive bones, will
outlive mine. Now in its
age, it protests the brace
of stone, seeks something
more like the kiss of bone.

House Keeping

I live in a house of obsolescence, with sideboards
and fire screens, doilies, traycloths, sherry glasses,
and china bowls made to serve food I'll never eat.

They are not heirlooms left to me by maiden aunts,
or Grandmothers who knew better days, but they
anchor me to this place more than bricks and mortar;

worry me more than mortgage payments and comfort
me more than central heating. When I touch them
they give off faint scents of beeswax, lavender, starch,

transporting me to where the Devil is bested every day
by never idle hands, and servant girls cut wafers of Godliness
from blocks of pink soap, before breaking their fast.

Speckless

was what she aimed for. Speckless floors and
windows but especially sheets, plunged

again and again into water hot as she could
make it, soap and scrub, knuckles raw,

twisting out the dead watery weight of them,
stinging in arms and shoulders; then again

through the wringer. Then watched like a
hawk for the shadow, the sniff of rain.

The inelegant dash to rescue them from
the deluge. Then in off the line to dance

them into narrow folds. Edge to edge, face
to face, hands almost but not quite touching,

chaste and white and clean smelling.
Something formal, a word you have read

but don't quite understand, gavotte or pavane.
Then the disinterring of the ironing cloths,

grey blankets laid on the table, old linen
smooth and scorched. The good day's work

of piles of speckless sheets growing and growing
at the uncovered end of the scrubbed table.

Clearances

For a whole summer my father worked
somewhere between a crying shame and

a mortal sin. Riding off every morning
to join the other hobnailed pillagers, stripping

and ripping out huge plaster ceiling roses
bordered with ivy and vines, chipping away

at deep cornices and elegant picture rails,
carting off loads of woodworm pitted

mahogany newel posts, sweeping up acres
of chandelier glass and oil lamp pendants.

In the evenings he conjured for us fabulous
tales of spoiled and rotting opulence: brocade

curtains hanging in ribbons, Persian carpets
mildewed and stinking, stained glass bleeding

into skips. Some things he couldn't help but
rescue: stilts, a doll's house with real wallpaper,

an improbable rusty sword, and best of all
thick rolls of draughtsman's paper where I drew

the family trees of ancient European royalty,
Ferdinand, Isabella, their not-yet-doomed daughters.

Oncoming Traffic

Although I'm middle-aged, my father still
warns me about the traffic; hates the loop
of my daily walk, which is not a level path
following Malahide strand as it becomes
Portmarnock, or the tree enclosed stroll
though the castle; but a gasping, almost run,
up and down hill, along a busy road, the uncut
verges creating blind corners, leaving only
a narrow space to squeeze myself into, away
from the rushing cars. He says Downpatrick
paths are rough and all aslant; wearing out shoes
too quickly, forcing your feet into unusual angles.

In vain, I tell him up and down hill is better
for the lungs, the joints; pumps blood more
efficiently, makes me fitter. That I always face
the oncoming traffic, never go that way in
the dark. He goes on fretting; the boy racers,
the men in white vans, mobiles clamped
to their ears, the women checking their mirrors
for sleeping babies. They don't care about me,
would see me in the ditch. He does, however,
admit the yellow gorse that I now call whins,
the Meadowsweet and dog roses, the wild
honeysuckle, missing from his walks for years.

Blue

Some women swore by razor blades,
hoarded in sweet tins and cups. Hovered
over husbands shaving in small mirrors,
terrified they would discard the blunt.
Others were faithful to nails and hinges;
on Sunday walks scouring shorn ground
for treasure. A discarded bolt a triumph.
Those were the days our mothers took
up hems, stretched mince. But never
gave in to soil. Every year the sowing
of rusty metal. The keeping of hydrangeas
impossibly blue.

Grand National

This is a day for print, blackening
our fingers, smudging the lines

we trace from garish colours, through
form, weight, odds. The paper should

be broadsheet, stretched on the kitchen
table, so we all can see, little ones hoisted

up to make their choices. This is the day
we take out of our fathers' toolboxes,

words we will not use until next year,
tongue tie, chevron, unseated, yielding.

We work out stakes on pages torn from
copy books, pour scorn on nephews

who suggest popcorn for the main event,
for this is permanently 1972 or 3; colour tv

is a novelty, the only acceptable refreshments
are tea, Miwadi, buttered fruit cake.

This is the day we first understand winning
and losing, the futility of relying on others,

the randomness of history, the results
of bad choices, everyday injustice.

Wedding China

My mother's wedding tea set
sits on my second-hand dresser,

bought cheaply to fill a space,
when the marital dresser went

to another house, along with its
collection of jointly chosen delph.

She gave me the china to fill
the gaps, dress the empty shelves

with colour; pale primrose yellow
with gold trim on the delicately

fluted edges of the plates and
saucers. The pattern is a flower

of a deeper yellow, edged with red.
It is a proper tea set with a lidded

sugar bowl and small cream jug.
They were never intended for use,

those tea sets, but were essential
to the wedding list, along with bales

of towels, eiderdowns, canteens
of cutlery. In my childhood, women

whispered enviously of sets of sheets
from Switzer's, apostle and egg spoons.

I prefer my mother's tea set to the one
that sat on the other dresser, its lustre

and delicate primrose yellow, its edge
of gold, pattern of red, the flower that

can't be found in any plant catalogue.
It looks just as wedding China should.

Boxed Up

I take the black pencil skirt, a ruffle
running almost the whole length of it,
from the box. Folded into tissue paper
so we might dream ourselves in a line
of women who regularly waited for
boxes from fashionable dress shops;
unwrapping bright silks, delicate lace.
The word 'trousseau' comes to mind.

What I think of is my great-grandmother,
one of those girls living in box rooms.
Boiling under the eaves of a Chicago
townhouse, the summer heat rising and
rising until it finds her sunk in an old
mattress. Her wardrobe a cardboard
suitcase; one good dress, boots stuffed
with yesterday's newspaper.

The best cast-offs parcelled up for home.
A black astrakhan coat with jet buttons,
shoes with buckles, dresses made from
crepe-de-chine, poplin, lawn. And tucked
away, maybe in a pocket, the envelope
of dollars to feed the cattle her sisters-in-law
would milk, their feet easing into the dew
soaked grass she seeded.

I imagine her at the attic window, trying
to match the colour of her childhood
sky as expertly as she matched thread,
her fingers running over the tray of greys
in some emporium of plenty; or stopping
in front of a display of winter fashion, seeing
in the wool of a coat the exact swirling purple
mauve of the Reek in summer evening.

Beating the Enemy

Because the enemy was sly, apt
to hide in lazy mornings, a slightly
damp jumper worn to school, a vest
too soon brought in from the line;
she learned to scavenge and hoard.

Every stick passed on the road
could be broken to carry; branches
of fallen trees hidden until later, when
she would go back, balance them
on a plank placed across the pram.

Because disease was as close as a
neighbour, as familiar as family; even
tiny pieces of slack were tenderly piled
in a special corner of the shed, with
the solicitude birthing cats weren't given.

Yesterday's headlines were never
re-read, but became the tight twists
that breathed life into the dry wood
and precious coals, set them dancing
into every corner of the kitchen;

where, given half a chance, the black
damp would blind the windows,
drip down the walls, pool on the floor,
invade throats and chests, bloom
red on handkerchiefs and pillowcases;

send her hunting for the battered
suitcase, that she brought home
what remained of them: pyjamas,
shirts, a tattered teddy bear,
some odd shillings and pence.

Exhumation

These are the stories bones can tell:
that you were felled by a club,
split by a stone, pierced by an arrow,
stabbed with a sword.
That your ankle fractured more than once,
that you were worn down by
carrying heavy loads, or walking
again and again from place to new place.
That you had arthritis, leprosy, syphilis,
that you endured periods of hunger,
that you gave birth.
That you were a young woman, an old
man, a not yet fused-together child.

These are the stories bones can't tell:
that you stretched in the sun like a cat,
scooped snow into your mouth,
dug a hole to bury childish treasure.
That it was your soul you reset
time after time, tying a splint to it
until it could bear your weight.
That your young mother bought
you forty frocks. That you might die
remembering your own child's
hands patting your face.
That in between there was
drought and thin harvests.

Waxing Old, a Distemper

'Dr Lister calls Pearls found in Muscles…the Distempers of Muscles waxing old.'
— Walter Harris, *The Antient and Present State of the County of Down*, 1744

Somewhere in the ooze and mud
you will step on its buckled, twisted

ridge. It will shrivel from your touch,
cleave hard to some rock. You will

prise it out, defy the watchers, secrete
it in your pocket; this your fairytale;

the crone hunched in her distemper,
spinning straw into gold. This pearl,

as serene as silk, the exact, dense
velvet of the nativity sky. It will find

its way to a setting of silver, a clasp
of diamonds, silencing the rooms lit

by thousands of candles. Waxing old,
we are charmed by this story; still longing

for a hand to coax, someone to believe
our long-held-in words are treasure.

Forgetting the streets of idle shops,
the trays of other unsold lots; clumsy,

old fashioned, hard to shift; there no
longer being much of a market in pearls.

Wasp's Nest

If you could write on the paper
of a wasp's nest, what would
you write, a prayer for the torment
of stings and welts? Punishment
for when you took the brush handle,
smashed down the nest; claiming
fear, when what you really felt
was spite; the industry of the queen,
her precision which is really love;

the perfect nursery folds of the nest,
the snugness of its fit under the eaves
of the summer house, playhouse,
pretend house; thirty feet from the
main house, playhouse, pretend house;
its concrete blocks trimmed with red
brick and rendered, which is another
way of saying pebble-dashed, which
is another way of saying dashed.

In the Utility Room

In troublesome times find sanctuary;
round tower or pit, the bottommost
cabin of a ship. Take to the empty road
with your empty purse, your suitcase
full of the wrong season's clothes.

In troublesome times hide yourself,
in the narrowest room of the house;
barely space for the ironing board,
the sweep of your arm over blouses,
shirts, the line's companion pieces.

Consider the black and white cows
considering the sky; the blueness
of the world, its greenness, the nearby
yellow whins, the fading memory
of the last cries of their calves.

Concentrate on the smell of clean
cotton rising with the steam, the speed
with which you whip through pillowcases,
the arms of the shirts neatly folded over
the place where their hearts might be.

For My Son: A Weather Eye

On the way home the weather changes,
the wind hums a faint Sunday hymn,

and in the small hotel behind green
corrugated sheds, there is a wedding.

Who gets married on a Sunday evening,
so far from anywhere but the road to

and from the ferry? We can't see the
bride. The guests are middle-aged,

heavy-set; the women, bulk balanced
on kitten heels, are in flowered dresses

made for the young, the slim. They
belong in heavy coats, heather mix,

with gleaming buttons, should carry
handbags whose clasps click, opening

on folded handkerchiefs, Fox's
Glacier Mints. They look like aunts,

perhaps they are, the unseen bride, slip
of a girl, a dead's sister's child (the flighty one);

wearing a dress they picked out, launched
into married life, on this windy night,

to a bridegroom they picked out. Solid
like them, ballast, to stop her drifting

out to sea. And here on the ferry road
miles from where I've left my son,

beginning a different life, I want to beg
of them to keep on him, a weather eye.

Booley House

Step on step. On lintel
balance; under your thin
summer shoes those bumps
are hearthstones, thresholds;
sinking further every year.

Soon you will be taller
than their doors, their gable
ends; then past the game of
choosing the highest house
with the best view, over the sea,

the shrinking fields, the dots
of sheep. The one with the
widest window sill, a worn
smooth groove where you lie
and imagine their climb

to the sweeter grass.
Nearer the sun; warming
cold bones, greening
their winter world. Free
from scouring, hoarding.

Who cares about dust
in summer dwellings,
gaps in doorways, loose
panes of glass, smoking
chimneys, empty sacks?

And I will learn to make
that summer ascent, live
in seasons; divide my world
into your going away,
your coming back.

Unhinged

It is the fragile ribbon that holds
everything together; carved ribs
of ivory, convent lace, the smoothest,
silk; the very mechanism of fold
and unfold. Without it the ribs unhinge,

find themselves in rusty biscuit tins,
mixed in with postcards telling of trains
to be met; brooches with no pins.
The carver's teeming dreams of vine
and fern clogged with grease and dust.

Childish fingers poke into the leaves,
worrying tiny holes between rose
and hearts' ease. The busy enterprise
of the fan; ivory hunter, Chinese carver,
Belgian nun is long bankrupt.

With care and the exact breadth
and weave of ribbon you can rethread
the fan. It will work almost like new,
fold and unfold; but what would you do
with it, your dancing days far behind you?

ACKNOWLEDGEMENTS

Acknowledgements are due to the following publications in which versions of some of these poems first appeared: *1798: Our Shared Heritage*; *A New Ulster*; *The Bangor Literary Journal*; *The Blue Nib*; *Crannóg; Dodging the Rain; FourXFour; The Honest Ulsterman; How can life go on: Poems and Prose for Holocaust Memorial Day, 2017*, (Lagan Online)*; Mary Evans Library Poems and Pictures Blog; The North; Resonance* (Community Arts Partnership)*; Poetry Ireland Review;* and *Skylight 47.*

Thanks to author Patricia Byrne (*The Preacher and the Prelate*, Merrion Press), who allowed me to share the reference to Eliza Nangle's letter about the Achill Mission in 'Mission'.

I am very grateful to all at Doire Press, especially John Walsh and Lisa Frank for the publication and production of this book and to the Arts Council of Northern Ireland for supporting it. Thanks also to Tríona Walsh for the cover design.

Thanks to Olive Broderick, Colin Dardis and Moyra Donaldson for reading the poems and commenting on them.

Thanks also to all the poets who have supported my work, including members of Women Aloud Northern Ireland (WANI), and members of Words for Castleward Writing Group and especially Olive Broderick, Colin Dardis and Geraldine Dardis O'Kane. Thanks to Jill Kerr for encouraging me to go to a creative writing class.

I am especially grateful to my family for their support of my writing and for inspiring many of these poems.

LINDA MCKENNA was brought up in Kinsealy in North County Dublin and educated at Malahide Community School, Trinity College Dublin and the University of Leicester. Following six years spent working in Leicester, she moved to Northern Ireland in 1993, and has lived in Downpatrick for over twenty years.

Linda began writing in 2015 and has had poems published in a variety of journals. In 2018 she won the Seamus Heaney Award for New Writing and the Red Line Book Festival Poetry Competition. Her work has also been shortlisted for the 2017 Eyewear Twelve Poems for Christmas competition and highly commended in the 2018 Over the Edge New Writer of the Year Competition. This is her first collection.